Watermarks

September 12
2008

Watermarks

EVERYTHING!

for
Maureen
& Tom too

Poems by Joanne Page

PEDLAR PRESS | Toronto

Love
Joanne

ACKNOWLEDGEMENTS
The publisher wishes to thank the Canada Council for the Arts and the Ontario Arts Council for their generous support of our publishing program.

LIBRARY AND ARCHIVES CANADA
CATALOGUING IN PUBLICATION

Page, Joanne--
Watermarks / Joanne Page.

Poems.

ISBN 978-1-897141-23-6

I. Title.

PS8581.A383W37 2008 C811'.54
C2008-903855-X

COVER ART Joanne Page

DESIGN Zab Design & Typography, Toronto

TYPEFACE Baskerville

Printed in Canada

The Canada Council for the Arts since 1957 | Le Conseil des Arts du Canada depuis 1957

ONTARIO ARTS COUNCIL
CONSEIL DES ARTS DE L'ONTARIO

for Anna

Contents

Beloved of the Sky

12 A Brief History of Snow
27 Sir John A. Macdonald's Last Season

Freeze-Frame

36 The Turning
38 Unsigned, Under Glass

Nature Morte
51

From the Hitherto Unpublished Journals of Miss Byrdie T., Inveterate Traveller and Champion of Lost Causes

72 Bay of Quinte

74 Walden Pond

75 Kiloho Bay Hawaii

76 East Arm Temagami

79 Lake Huron

80 Ryoanji Temple Kyoto

81 Tributary West Credit River

82 Assateague Channel Virginia

83 Bow River

85 Desperation Lake NWT

86 Sondrestrom Fjord

87 Illulissat Harbour
89 Davis Strait
91 Baffin Bay
93 Pond Inlet

Cloud
97

103 Notes

Beloved of the Sky

A Brief History of Snow

Saved By

In BC four hundred and something he sets forth
from Thurium with the notebook that will become
his little-known tenth History. He goes upriver
to a confusion of stopped tributary streams, and people,
a dwarf race dressed in skins who walk on crystal.
Their ways, he reports, are cloaked, their worship
hidden. From the sky white dust falls without end.
Herodotus is not amazed, merely cold. He leaves,
a struck bell peals in the valley. He will send
no word to Pericles of such bleakness.

That's It in a Hazelnut

Downtown Norwich and Julian's unfailing good humour 13
is tested through another round of bubonic plague. Half
a mile away by the river, Lollards burn in the Lollards Pit.
Soon the peasants will revolt but, never fear, all shall
be well and all shall be and so on, until cooped up
in her anchorhold, she snaps. No one will ever know
that, far from devotional, the famous *That It Is So*
Without End is scribbled down in a freak May storm.

Mark You

Inuit are born, a blue spot at the base of their spine.
They grow to have straight black hair, small feet
and hands, sturdy trunk and body mass adapted
to cold. Their language lives. Last year they made
two snow words into *silajua pigalavja* meaning
ozone layer. This year both are in grave danger.
Now they need words for shrinking sea ice,
emissions, tar sands runoff and glacial retreat.
Seasonal adjustments call for more green terms.
They say a bear's fur yellows when she starves.

White

Pigment, writes Cennini in Il Libro dell' Arte, comes *15*
in little cakes like goblets or drinking glasses. The more
you grind the more perfect the colour. Pliny's came
from Rhodes. Lead and vinegar. Perfectly deadly.
Vermeer mixed quartz and alabaster for his walls and
highlights. Paul Kane's fate: the endless winter of
the blind. Italian painters failed at the polar effect
whereas the Dutch excelled. Gwen John didn't try.
She turned to heat instead and took Rodin to bed.

Unlike Our Present Life

16 The war to end all wars and he is seventeen.
Arrives at Sayesette to lines of captured Jerries.
Mud and guns at night, gas is everywhere. Scarcity
of oats and hay. Two mules tethered to a nag's head
hitching post. One kicks him in the knee. *Wounded
in action* writes the hometown press and he will
favour the leg in nights ahead as weather unloads
on Russia, buries Chekhov's grave, storms west
to the front. As the white bird flies steadily inland.

Encore

His Holiness the 17th Karmapa with two friends
walks into exile over a mountain pass where parents
tie their children down when the big winds rise.
No witness but another snowfall. Before his time
the 11th Karmapa's birth brought rainbows,
drifts of flowers in winter and pails of water
turned to milk. I was born in a cattle byre,
says 17 K., and everything old is new again
such as borrowed water falling from above.

Wither?

18 They say it has no smell. Who would differ? Perhaps
Heitor Villa-Lobos at the window, drawn to the view
by its distant scent. Upon his music paper he scores
the mountain's shape and presto! Sweet melody.
Or Royal Marine Skyring sent from Darwin's Beagle
to lay claim. Tierra del Fuego for the Union Jack!
Marooned. On the island he left a small account
on parchment in a box: *The jeezling cold were not to*
be borned, the forking sleet were the pong of Father's
socks and I were ready to die. God Save the King.

Ah Spring

Cholera is rampant in London. Folk drop like flies. *19*
Dr. John Snow, using his noggin, maps the cases,
finds they cluster close to the Broad Street well.
In a swift and decisive practice of preventative
medicine, notes Rachel Carson with audible cheer,
he removes the handle from the pump. A moment
of hope in her book on poison. Forgive Rachel
her gloom. When she came to see birds were dead
she betook herself to her cold and empty bed.

Taking the Cross

20 Crusading, some thirty thousand children
follow the boy Stephen of Cloyes to Marseilles
where the sea is supposed to part. It does not.
Instead the aptly named Hugh the Iron
and William the Pig hire seven vessels
and ship them into slavery. Peter the Hermit,
on the other hand, has a grand time though
not through personal charm. Swarthy with a
donkey's face he barnstorms barefoot overland
until his rabble army falls to the Turks.
Up to his ears in Scottish weather, Edward
of England at the mercy of whiteouts and drifts
misses his boat altogether.

The Canon

The literature of snow is simple enough for fools.
Like most its origin is oral, flake to flake you
might say. Largely Os and Us, its books have
a certain sameness making interpretation a matter
of conjecture. Authority of authorship has a similar
shifting nature blowing, as it were, in the wind.
Historical texts include those on Sugaring Off
in the Maple Bush and Home of the Penguin.
Tomes on Siberia have been withdrawn whereas
the permafrost set will soon be remaindered.

21

Pure as the Driven

22 And just as easy to come by if you know where.
At Suzhou, in *The Garden to Linger In,* beneath
a light dusting, a scholar rock known as Cloud-Capped Peak
adjusts its awkwardness. What is its secret? If tapped
the rock will ring? What the gazing scholar
sees: within the highest mountain a cave, within
the cave a stalactite giving only one drop once,
a nectar known as kindness. Deep snow
meditation in China, the world entire.

Exit Eden

If they had owned snowshoes it might have been
different. Contrary to popular belief it was not
the apple incident but the heavy accumulations
and prolonged cold snap that sent them packing.
Serpent and fruit a cover story they cooked up.
The matter was matter, not morals.
In fact the days of wine and roses were under
a good six feet and the Almighty a mite red-
faced at mixing up the climate zones.

Upstairs at the Dickinson's

24 Storm-stayed in Amherst. Guess whose nose
presses on the pane? The Belle rummages
in her mind for a little fugue on infinity.
Wild night after wild night of spangled air
and woolly lawn. She may lose her mind.
Riven, she pens lines of love for two,
for Master and for Sue (how glittering
they shone). Sun fills up the room.
Suddenly the snow is gone.

Visitations

Now and then through long nights
when tracking is best the Woodland
Cree come upon a set of footprints
incised in an otherwise unmarked
carpet of deep snow. Starting nowhere
going nowhere. Beginning and end
without the journey. As if the walker
had been issued from the sky then
reabsorbed. Traceless.

Rewrites

26 Children's stories, of course, derive
from Ice Age tales. As years wore on
people tinkered with them. Originally
the old woman who had so many children
she didn't know what to do never lived
in a drafty shoe. They would have frozen
solid. Instead her mob thrived in caribou skin.
As for Goldilocks her bears were white.
Cinderella shovelled snow instead of ash.
And so on. You can imagine!

Sir John A. Macdonald's Last Season

The long winter arrives early and stays late.
For weeks no one remembers seeing the sun.
Or stars at night. Hail or sleet or driving snow
Obscures the sky. Snow lays itself down in
Archeological layers over the mica mines
Near Sydenham and the lockmaster's house
At Kingston Mills. Near Jones Falls it stops up
The blacksmith's stack filling the forge with smoke.
The lake freezes to unusual depth giving off
Detonations in the dark. Ice throws up its glittering
Wall along the waterfront. Snow heaps itself
Halfway up doors and first floor windows
Until the city seems to sink into the white earth,
The spires of St. Mary's and St. George's last to go.

28 Wind flings titanic drifts against the walls
Of the Asylum then disperses snow over
The great prairie of frozen lake. Snow
Entombs carelessly tended dogs and horses
As well as the bees in hives on William Street.
Small trees disappear. Overburdened branches
Snap from the oldest maples. Birds die
Like seedpods. Snow imprisons the elderly
And small children. Maids and boys labour
Ceaselessly shifting snow while yet more falls.
Streets dwindle to rutted tracks too narrow
For horse-drawn sleighs. Trips outside to wells
And backhouses become polar expeditions
Undertaken only in cases of dire need.

Into this foul season the Old Chieftain comes 29
To fight his last campaign. By CPR he crawls
From London to Strathroy. Crowds with fireworks
And torches light his snowy way. From open carriage
To steamy town halls he pleads for his Dominion:
As for myself my course is clear. British I was born
And British I shall die. Ailing he struggles on.
St. Mary's Acton Guelph: his speech the same. *With*
Reciprocity the Grits will sell us out. In Oakville
Beneath the Union Jack he warns of annexation
Waiting in the wings. Weather darkens, worsens.
Seventy-six and ill he will not see summer.
Toronto and west to Martin's Opera House.
Collapse. Just nine days left but he is spent.

30 By the Fifth of March social calls stop.
The outlying villages of Portsmouth and
Barriefield lacking current political news
Subside into argument and recapitulation.
Skeins of geese fly above in dimness.
Cardinals whistle spring songs but still
The unending season rolls out in brittle
Nerves and lost business. Snow creeps down
Necks up sleeves into boots and gloves
Until it seems in the moments before dawn
On this the morning of the mid-winter vote
To work its way under the skin
And into the vessels of the body and
Chambers of the disordered mind
In thick infusions of frigid misery.

Now the sun rises. First a burn of red 31
At the horizon. Then the clear sky inclines
Amber now gold. Trees throw shadows.
Pale mauve and pink hollow into the piles
Of dirty snow which begin to glisten as the sun
Appears over the Fort. Yellow light swoons
Over the city. Bars of it pierce windowpanes
Turning furniture into polished ore. Buildings
Take bold shapes with fierce black edges.
Under the glacier of Earl Street warm air
Coaxes trickles of meltwater into a creek
That runnels sharply downhill. Crevasses
Open in lake ice suddenly. Snow avalanches
Off the steeply pitched roof of the Piano Works.

32 In days the streets teem with commerce.
Once again horses draw farm wagons to town
Moving lumber to the kilns behind the Works
Cheese boxes and shingles from Bellrock mill
At Depot Creek to city stores. Stranded
Travellers pour out of stuffy hotel lodgings
Into the warming air. Stray wayfarers
Irish workers and thrifty Scottish merchants
Seethe along the muddy boardwalks. Trains
Move feldspar from Sydenham to water's
Edge for trading to the South. Released
From winter bondage the streets heave
And shift beneath their crystalline covering
As the frost departs from the earth.

As spring takes hold the Chieftain weakens further.
He takes the vote but winning brings him down.
Four hundred and eighty-three loyal ballots
Return him to the Hill but cannot save him. By
June he is gone. Then once again by train
To Kingston and slow procession through
The city of his young manhood in company
Of many who loved him and some who did
Not through his long hurrah. Now laid to rest
As the crowd begins to grumble about trade
With the Yanks. Graft and corruption
In the capital. The weather the weather!
Mildly unsatisfied. Politely so. National
Character fully formed. His work done.

Freeze-Frame

The Turning

On the surface, lakewater heated all summer by sun
gradually cools, becomes denser, sinks like lost love
to depths leaving warm water in its place that will in
turn cool, become heavy, subject to gravity. Really
it's the moon's doing. The molecular motion
slows and molecules part to form the precise lattice,
with hollow centre, that make ice crystals (*crystal*
from the Greek meaning *clear ice*). Now the entire
body will forfeit what reserve heat it holds to rise
in great vaporous breaths, mighty sighs you may
read as a sign that the lake has taken leave
of its senses or gone boiling mad if you did not
know latitude or the temperament thereof.

Without wind the crystals slowly form.
Look! An ice needle shoots out, stops,
then one takes off on the bias, yet another
backs over itself until the surface is quilted,
cross-stitched with silver, each sewn patch
solidifies, and the skim is thin as skin.
And if the cold snap holds, the brittle
surface deepens, keeping the water's final
writing within itself like paper holds watermark,
pedigree and history of origins under your feet:
sealed, secure, legible. Kneel and see.

Unsigned, Under Glass

Origin 1

There is little to go on. The many paintings, of course,
But she never caught his interest as a subject. A few
Photographs remain, daguerreotypes in the first instance
Such as the Cobourg house of a master cabinetmaker
Who is presently working on a rosewood desk with
Bird's-eye drawers, assisted by an itinerant Irish artist,
Craftsman hungry for travel and fame. These are bygone days
So a horse-drawn carriage blocks our view of its gracious
Entrance though the unusual detail around the door marks
The home as one of the town's finest. The owner has
Eight children, four of each. The oldest paints according
To the limits of her life, scenes and flowers. Presently
She is preserving plums in glass jars in the kitchen on the
Right, behind the line of trees. She is bored beyond words.

Reversal 2

In the parlour she poses in fussy dark taffeta.
Hair pinned behind her ears, a dark layered bonnet
Coiling her head like a cobra. By the look of her –
Stern mouth, piercing eyes, head turned, chin up –
She might be reserved by nature or merely looking the
Oldest daughter. In fact she is seething. Just now
The gentleman artist with whom she thinks she is a little
In love has taken off giving only his burning passion
For pigment and Rome as reason, leaving her father
Shorthanded. Leaving her in the lurch. Ahead lies her
Mother's life cut down to fit her like last year's gown.
In *his* photo, had there been one, you would see New
Orleans dimly out the door of the crowded room he
Calls a studio. If you could hear there would be music.

Debut 3

Taken from the local paper, a rendering of her work
Said to be bought for a private collection, oil study
Of men outside a tavern, well-to-do by their dress,
Raising tumblers of some drink, probably ale. So
Daring, a young woman painting likenesses
Of gents at leisure. Scandalizes the sewing circle.
She does not give a fig. She has her reasons. One
Is the postcard from Genoa, a jaunty note signed
With a single flourished letter as if there were no other
She might know by such initial. As if she were waiting.
An armchair critic writes that though the painted men
Are stiff the landscape offers promise and the glass
Vessels are handled deftly enough to be painted in
Dutch, peculiar words of praise she dwells on.

Excursion 4

Finds her alone before Colborne Lodge, a *cottage*
Ornée in the city. The owner-architect works in his
Den labouring at drawings for a contest to build
The Lunatic Asylum on Queen Street. Previous
To his career as builder he was drawing master at
The College for Boys which is how he came to know
Her painter. Who has not yet returned from his pro-
Longed infatuation with high art. Why is she waiting?
No one can say. To date she has turned down seven
Proposals of marriage. In fairness none appeal. To
Pass the weeks she makes small pictures of still
Life arrangements, jars and bottles. She has come
To town to hear the famous author Charles Dickens
With her least favourite but only unmarried sister.

Studies 5

42 Here at last is a glimpse of him very blurred but
Recognizable in the door to the National Gallery
London England where he is pursuing his passion
As has been his custom, copying masterworks
Day by day, Signorelli's muscled frescos at Orvieto,
Delacroix in Paris, portraits portraits portraits, today
A Raphael. Marathons of underpainting, glazes,
Shading, meticulous technician searching for
His subject which he is beginning to suspect awaits
Him where he came from. He will not give up
Or give in quite yet. Tomorrow he has arranged to
Meet the American newly the toast of the town
Owing to his pictures of the North West that have
Caught on like wild fire. The Last Frontier is in.

Unsigned 6

Of three women before an art exhibit. The First
Annual show. The men were photographed on
Their own, the larger group, nearly everyone,
Let's face it. She has declined the photo. Indeed
Has caused quite a stir over the attribution of her
Picture refusing the usual way: By a Lady. Wants her
Name used and the others' too. Like men. For
Reasons she expounded to the women as the men
Declined to listen or laughed. There was also the
Problem of the glass. Where were the flowers, the
Sunny scenes? She is out of sorts on all fronts. He
Is returned and intends some wanderings is how he
Puts it. It may be the time has come to end this the
Longest courtship, though, wait, he says, please.

Articles 7

44 The harbour, the pier, the lighthouse, a calm day.
Hers the figure walking away. Invisible in her hand
His tiny photo taken between the second and third
Trip. Resplendent, really, in his buckskin fringed
Jacket, one arm off-camera holding a paddle or
Musket, something long. Hair wild, beard roughly
Trimmed. Beads here and there. What will it come
To, his brave travels, the notebooks and the many
Artifacts? Meanwhile her dowry amasses as do
The hourglasses she paints and stores away. He
Writes: Yesterday we shot the Dalle de Mort
Most dangerous of all the western river rapids
And I thought of you. And if you had drowned,
She says aloud, what of all you missed with me?

Industry 8

The famous shot. The patron with the painter.
Really he is up against it having undertaken
Many dozens of paintings to be complete in short
Order, mere years. The painter's reach exceeds
His prodigious brush. His industry knows no
Bounds. Frenzy in the studio. Pressure from
Without. That he is the most famous tourist yet
Known in the land affords him nowhere to hide
And whose fault be that? To boot he will write
His memoir, flog it in England and become
A best-selling author. Any sane soul would
Wonder how a single man might do so much
Alone. However you may see the paintings for
Yourself if you care to. Note the many details.

Arrangement 9

At last. The wedding party though small seems
Pleased. The groom in black, bride in cream.
Lilac clouds the garden. Children all lined up,
Cousins to the four children she will bear, two
Of each. Her life of waiting ends. In a new city
House family and work under one roof will unite
Them as he juggles the obligations he has arduously
Struggled to accumulate. Travel's grueling pace
Has exhausted him. Vision fading, he is harried.
Young men petition at the door for instruction.
Will he never have peace! This being speculation
We might wonder if she escaped her mother's life
After all. As for her longing, it may be sealed,
Its many reflective surfaces scratched and dull.

Canvas 10

The row house on Wellesley Street, Toronto.
Worried children and the blind sleep lightly.
They wake to the smell of turpentine. A nearby
Crowd of songbirds begins its dawn chorus.
The boy sits upright in bed, considers the crown
Of his brother's head. Night business of the
House does not concern him nor lantern glow
Beneath the bedroom door. He knows what his
Mother does. The volume of his father's misery
Presses air from the rooms making each breath
Hard to draw. Today he will go with him to the
Island with sketching book and pans of colour.
At home the last great painting begins to assert
Itself: *Encampment at River's Edge in Snow.*

Collection 11

48 A stone museum crouches on the west side
Of the grand avenue, enormous reliquary of the
Past, its guardians scurrying from hall to hushed
Hall with visible purpose, ignoring the elderly
Woman and her large family evidently of no
Account. They, in turn, do not care. They come
For the pictures as they do each year to mark
The date of his passing, to honour the flight
Of his fancy. She stands a little apart, away
From the casual words of their dear voices.
They ignore the tears coursing down her
Soft cheeks. She will come alone when they
Lose interest or move away, until her death
In the year the young Dominion loses its Chief.

Unknown 12

Glossy catalogue reproduction in full colour,
Identified in the accompanying text: *To be*
Sold at auction, unusual series of small
Still life paintings, mid-nineteenth century,
Unsigned, each an arrangement of glassware,
In some cases containing clear liquids, perhaps
Water, others identifiably hourglasses
Full of fine sand. The brushwork more than
Accomplished, deftly coloured textures
Breathtakingly luminous, brilliant studies
Evoking the heyday of the Flemish masters.
Could only have been painted by a superb
Early colonial artist, perhaps Fowler
Or Armstrong, though his forté was fruit.

Nature Morte

The Cellular Memory
of Paint:

a painter's hand,
the painter's touch.

Brush breath on the pear
burns it gold

advancing the glowing shapes
by saturation,

laying white into the lily
tiny furrows of luster

through the underpainting
oyster shells, burrs of light.

Stippled edge of stone
point, point, weight and heft.

Behind, beneath
the many varnished layers

darker deeper
richest hyacinth.

Its assertion:
immortal bosc and stone
and flower outlive us,
pigment's ever after.

To Black

Darksome Lord
midnight owl on your shoulder
in a veiled world.

Mystic!

Master of outline,
edger of shape,
stroke by stroke
and then
in one fell swoop
end the tale.

You are secrecy
beguiling,
bloodstone

unseen at
the centre
of dark need.
You are the
undiscerned,
what is forgotten,
the abyss.

Rarest onyx
all-seeing
pupil in the eye.

Coal and char
lead and soot,
light swallowed
whole.

To Brown

Humility itself.
You are terrestrial
gravity, slow to declare yourself,
impossible to provoke.

You hide yourself
behind leaves,
in the blessed
umber earth.
Reliable
loyal,
your sienna
self everywhere,
broadcast
planetary hue,
model citizen.

Bearer of growing things,
home to burrowers,
rising in dry
season
as a plume
of memory.

O fur
and feather,
chestnut burnished,
tanned fragrance
often overlooked,
second last chapter
lost book.

58 Murmured words,
hushed aside,
natural gestures.
Averted gaze.
Calm.
Unseen for days.

Shadowy remembered place
that says you must begin again.

To Red

Rigamarole of crimson
like flame
you cannot be broken
only smothered
or dowsed,

you are pulsing
utility of the heart's
brilliant reach.
Bestride the prism.
Unmatched, ill-fated
you take the day.

60 You burn like a cheap candle,
melt all over the table,
run ahead like spirits
to the inferno
and throw yourself
on the fire.

Scarlet scandal,
arterial spectre
you are blazing.
Go higher,
go faster.

To Green

Most difficult.
A trial you are,
terre-verte,
you would test
the patience
of yon saint.

Jealous rival,
jaded.
Peacock,
every scene
a portrait sitting,
a burial,
a germinating seed.

62 You are your second nature.
Mistress of fertility
you defy
reproduction.
Restless,
vine and stalk,
tendrils creeping,
there is no stopping you,
you madden and delight.

Eden's wild runaway,
you enslave
at every turn.
Enthralled
how I hunger for you.

To Blue

That fills the cobalt waves.
That emboldens flags and rules.
That sees the forest felled.
That slakes thirst.

That crowns the jewel.
That dusts the plum skin.
That crepes death's door.
That pays the ferryman.
That takes the lash.

That travels with the dawn.
That robes the virgin.
That beds the starry night.
That sinks the prize.
That steals the show.

64 That will rise and fall and rise again.
That seeks level ground.
That engulfs the void.

That will pass and pass
Until there is no more.

To Gold

It would seem
you have much to answer for.

Forsaking all others,
deep within your
fierce brassy spell,
knaves and fools
devote their waking hours
pursuing only you.

Scoundrels court your
heavenly hue
of bells and haloes,
traders slaughter
to hide the secret
at the centre of the crocus.

66 Empress,
how you toy with our mortal selves,
fill us with desire
for your midday topaz heat,
afternoon's intoxicating
mango flesh.
I cannot get my fill of you.

At the threshold of disaster
you relent,
soften into lamplight
in the window
at the end of the long
road to love.

To White

Simple story made of longing.
Elemental, textured, true.

Ivory, pure,
the lily's satin gown,

spider threads trim
its fading hem.

With all his flesh of zinc
beneath his snug skin

with every fibre
of his core,

68 Romeo secluded with his Juliet
in celibate eternity

together on the glowing floor.
Crystal arch, distant temple pale:

phantom sketches put aside.
One final wisp, bristled touch.

Done.
The painter lifts her brush.

From the Hitherto Unpublished Journals of Miss Byrdie T., Inveterate Traveller and Champion of Lost Causes

Bay of Quinte

You are mistaken when you say of water we have enough,
the woman says from the floor of the freshwater colloquium
in the lakeside motel at Belleville. She takes a breath,
she starts again: *the future will be written in water,*
she pleads. We know, the scientists interrupt, of course!
The politician nods. A local farmer, his neck wreathed
in bulbs of garlic, rolls his eyes as all resume the battle
of watery jurisdictions. Her mike goes dead in this old
Cassandra tale of those who find the trough then never drink.

She tires of visions, she tells the garlic farmer at the break,
is sick of hectoring. She wants to be voiceless, rid of prophecy.
Remember, he says, Socrates' advice to Ion:
the poet is light, winged and holy, there is no invention
in him until he has been inspired out of his sense,
and has no mind. She does not ask *what about the women*
for, oh! what suddenly she sees is people on beaches
and water drawing back. *There will first be too much,*
then too little, she says. Have a coffee, says the farmer.

Walden Pond

Ringed with rentable trailers, the water fouls its sands.
Nearby the windows in Emerson's house hoard their incisions,
Hawthorne's diamond scratchings on the upstairs pane,
skate marks on new ice. If not now when, if not you who,
my dear, my darling, so many miles so much clear road.
I have left my laugh in a jar set on the doorstep in case you come by.

When the day comes, sweet one, I will walk by the pond
in shadows and think of you arriving, when the day comes,
sweet one, I will pile up my life in you as in love transcendent.
Patron saint of those in danger of death by drowning,
think of your life as a brief summer. This is late August. Hurry.

Kiloho Bay Hawaii

What luck for the fish of the fathomless deep, full of flame
retardants beneath their coat of scales, no danger of spontaneous
combustion in clear waters as the reef gets its daily chemical
infusion, runoff from the fairways, the manicured greens

carpeting black lava on the dry side of the big island.
Beyond, below, a drift of harmonic giants feed
on bioluminous plankton and algae, spiralling sparklers,
their pyrotechnics fuelled by oxygen in short supply

as the ocean heats and the whale must dive deeper to cool
the great engine of her body lest it cook her bones or blow her up
as she breeches, the humpback singing her song for the slow
burn of undershore coral and the ultimate island, earth.

East Arm Temagami

At the end of the trail, fingers blue
at the tips. Rain becomes snow.
Canoe off into the east arm.
The first whitecap washes
in over the gunwale.
One in the middle bails
and sings *you are my sunshine,*
her cerebral palsy in overdrive,
in half a foot of water,
dizzy and blue-lipped sick,
me in the stern, a novice in the bow,
we are broadside to the waves
and drifting, each stroke a sweep
to ride the crest
to stay afloat.
Shoreline gone.

Here I miss a stroke.
The next wave will swamp.
Here is your death;
now do you love water?
It gives, it takes,
its element
is motion.
Mine is time.

Cherry grain
my paddle's
woody heart,
ribbed canoe
of patched canvas,
surge or drop,
whatever saved us.

78 Washed away
to the stern:
the oldest words
to learn dying by.

Lake Huron

On the beach at Southampton the Misses Fouse,
Shearsby, Pecover, Frickleton and Swindle
spread out a meal of parsnip and sweet potato done up
with nutmeg on a blanket at sunset for my pleasure.

We suspect you know nothing about getting old
that we do not, they say, passing slices of pumpkin pie
to passersby as the sun goes down and fuchsia blossoms
float on air, tiny crinolined dancers.

Spare the captive, shoe the fugitive, feed the hungry,
I say, and watch the current. Where have you been
that brings you here as you are, they say, without knowing
everything depends on learning how to let go.

The lake rides one syllable in and the other one out,
leaving its water voice in the air, rising.

Ryoanji Temple Kyoto

The lessons stabbingly clear
when they come. Stone basin
for ritual cleansing, long-armed
dipper to one side. Inscription:

I learn only to be content.
Nearby the fifteen zen stones
float in their white gravel sea,
a raked riddle.

At the temple of the mandarin ducks
are you wayfarer or pilgrim?
And when the question is put,
have you answer?

Tributary West Credit River

Grandfather took his shovel and terraced the front field.
Where the creek parted the hill he planted thirty poplars,
upearthed one end of the croquet lawn for hybrid roses and glads
all of which grew and thrived. One day Grandfather put on a suit
and went to Montreal on business where he died, appendix,
leaving Grandmother at home with five under ten, four boys and Mother.

While Gran went to fetch him back by wood box in a CN baggage car,
her father, that is to say, Great-grandfather, got out his axe to fell
the poplars and turn the creek to a row of ponds where he scattered
goldfish like loose change before he fled to the back forty
where he lived in the bush for two weeks, unrepentant.

I remember flickers of tangerine, all I could find of the fish,
a fearful child out solo, borne on adult stories over cocktails
stirred with swizzle sticks. He did it from deafness they told me
when I asked why, my legs on fire with the oily vengeance of the ponds'
nettles that told me no, no he didn't, I cried. Grandmother rose and said,
He preferred ponds, and left.

Assateague Channel Virginia

Down the Atlantic flyway come the snow geese in multitudes.
From the roof of my car before dawn watching water pale with fowl
I am not alone, alas, and even through the racket of geese I hear:
Goddamnit, I oughta belt your ass, lookit Momma, he spilt the damn coke
I oughta left you with your daddy, you don't get more so don't ask.

At dawn the geese quit the open water, cacophony of splash and honk,
flying inland to gorge on corn farmers leave for them in fall.
Carloads of watchers disperse to plates of scrapple and grits
leaving me to gradual silence and sudden movement at ground level,
thorn tree alive with a thousand hummingbirds jewelled
in red and green, engines burning high octane fuel in a blur.

Next summer precisely at dawn on the second Wednesday in July
volunteer firemen will round up the world famous wild ponies
on their barrier island and we will watch them swim to shore
where they rest and feed before the old and ornery are auctioned off
but for one runaway, its head in our tent, hooves planted foursquare,
no last supper here, apples and carrots all over the beach: banquet.

Tributary West Credit River

Grandfather took his shovel and terraced the front field.
Where the creek parted the hill he planted thirty poplars,
unearthed one end of the croquet lawn for hybrid roses and glads
all of which grew and thrived. One day Grandfather put on a suit
and went to Montreal on business where he died, appendix,
leaving Grandmother at home with five under ten, four boys and Mother.

While Gran went to fetch him back by wood box in a CN baggage car,
her father, that is to say, Great-grandfather, got out his axe to fell
the poplars and turn the creek to a row of ponds where he scattered
goldfish like loose change before he fled to the back forty
where he lived in the bush for two weeks, unrepentant.

I remember flickers of tangerine, all I could find of the fish,
a fearful child out solo, borne on adult stories over cocktails
stirred with swizzle sticks. He did it from deafness they told me
when I asked why, my legs on fire with the oily vengeance of the ponds'
nettles that told me no, no he didn't, I cried. Grandmother rose and said,
He preferred ponds, and left.

Assateague Channel Virginia

Down the Atlantic flyway come the snow geese in multitudes.
From the roof of my car before dawn watching water pale with fowl
I am not alone, alas, and even through the racket of geese I hear:
Goddamnit, I oughta belt your ass, lookit Momma, he spilt the damn coke
I oughta left you with your daddy, you don't get more so don't ask.

At dawn the geese quit the open water, cacophony of splash and honk,
flying inland to gorge on corn farmers leave for them in fall.
Carloads of watchers disperse to plates of scrapple and grits
leaving me to gradual silence and sudden movement at ground level,
thorn tree alive with a thousand hummingbirds jewelled
in red and green, engines burning high octane fuel in a blur.

Next summer precisely at dawn on the second Wednesday in July
volunteer firemen will round up the world famous wild ponies
on their barrier island and we will watch them swim to shore
where they rest and feed before the old and ornery are auctioned off
but for one runaway, its head in our tent, hooves planted foursquare,
no last supper here, apples and carrots all over the beach: banquet.

Bow River

On the first page of his phone book:
during a flood do not put yourself in peril,
do not attempt to cross any flowing stream,
do not take a road you may get stranded on.
Stay out of water, do not call Disaster Services
unless you need help.

The day I heard him say *home* and knew my son meant
the mountains with ravens and their hoarse fly-by routines,
not here with me where he began,

in the flatland's heat. Here I paint a still life for the honey bee
in which the flowers break out of the barn, run riot in the pasture
in a game of frozen-tag. The bee is it. Cow vetch, coltsfoot,

butter-and-eggs, wild game in continental crush of heat,
greenhouse air drifting over pearly everlasting and
when it seems nothing will ever be home-free again, comes

my dog, eternal optimism, following me around, his toenails chittering
questions on the floor: where's food, what's next, when's the walk?
and I see it all boils down to your own version of The Deluge.

Desperation Lake NWT

When there's no facing it down or fencing it in,
when you can't be cured, when you discover yourself
among small rodents haring down a worn path
repeatedly signed *this way to the cliff*, when
you are the overheated one in a temperate zone
or fail to notice the boom of your voice loud
and off-key when the piece is over,

the last place you need is a quiet pond,
all reflection and echo, or a river's promise
of arrival. Grab field glasses for the long
view, a level for balance. Imagine yourself
small in a big landscape, say the tundra,
with its hundred thousand lakes, inch-high
flowers in unheard-of variety. Consider
being stuck with one. Now study the rock.
Faced with stone, not even the moon's might
can bring to ebb what never flowed.

Sondrestrom Fjord

At eleven light thickens to cream over rock cliffs,
below, water mattes to green, stripped of artifice,
pure purpose moves us north to the Arctic Circle.

Near midnight bands of gold finger through clouds
in from the southwest, winds roil up four foot swells,
a bowhead in one with a pack of seals bound for Sisimut.

Four plastic parrots sway on wire perches above the bridge
leftovers from a winter trip to The Tropics. *Amazon*, I say to them,
rainforest, steam. Qu-vai-unikumut, I say for myself,

meaning *feel deeply happy*.

Illulissat Harbour

We pitch and yaw in open water,
ice forest in sight against a parchment sky,
dominions of winter calving
off the great ice field at Illulissat in August.

We hurry to the deck in orange sea jackets
and winter gear, a flock of eager puffins,
our ship a company of pairs: Jesuits, cardiologists,
Sicilian sisters two by two, gay men,

Manhattan shrinks, handwriting analysts,
a couple of farmers from Komoka
as if Noah had assembled the passenger list
with a plan in mind to preserve some of the less
common specimens of the species by freezing.

88 Now we are eggs in a carton, a dozen at a time,
from the ship in red motorized rafts,
tiny scarlet spots among the continents of ice,
damp exhalations of frigid air coming off
each one like prehistoric breathing.

The boatman Gary stills the engine, we drift,
he tells a story of penguins in a row
on the ice cap at the water's edge in Antarctica
where the rest of the freshwater is stored,

all shuffling sideways until one is nudged off
for the waiting leopard seal so they can dive, and
we look at one another, we who are in opposing
rows, at the beginning of the world or the end.

Davis Strait

Here we go up the coast in company with floating archipelagos
borealis azure, parliaments of ice boating northwest to Canada,
lordly tourists, motherlands with hitchhikers, gulls, seals,
the occasional white bear, the world in a guise I had imagined
but did not know to be a question: If this is not your Eden
what is?

I would require seasons, five or six, and a book of words to use
with one set of meanings, I would need pure colour
in great sweeps as well as inside and underneath where
you don't expect it. Belief would take the form of tolerant irony,
say lapsed Quaker, lack temple priests and rules but one:
love when you can.

My Eden would run on marsh gas, on wind, be governed by those
who mean to save the world with zeal except for Texans or,

come to think of it, feminist collectives, its civic spaces
made of dance and song and public art of the impermanent kind
that announces itself by departing. My Eden would have some hot
dark nights,

insects, frogs, roosting orange birds, ripe fruit, free lunch,
stable money and hauls of harvest, fair play, invention,
clean wells, children in bed linen by open windows, and snow,
yes, now and then on the domed roofs of the capital, at the edge
of the night where the white bear swims on his back through the bright
sea of his hunt.

Baffin Bay

Pocked and rippled the great bergs sail forth
on their bands of neon melt. They are rose,

blue, green, even peach, a Fifth Avenue
of ice loosed in the Gulf Stream, in and out

of the fog they come and go, antique dreams
like the practice of high courtesy we now name love.

Overhead the dovkies, pint-sized beer cans with wings
in millions on their summer flight to Lancaster Sound.

Is this a lesson of emptiness or optics, the law of averages
or motion? We are dots on the deck of our shabby ship

in our so-called expedition gear, the boat a speck in a sea
of floating behemoths that can sink us by merely overturning

in a moment too small in time for history.
The only insanity is not to be afraid.

Beside me you want your car to appear on the next floe,
voyage of doom, you hiss, keys in your hand,

undone by magnitude of scale. *Voyage of light,*
I think, *a purchase on majesty.*

Pond Inlet

As for the wind it is a rover, a stranger come to town
barnstorming idle sled dogs chained together on the sand.
It howls at TV dishes, at snow machines:

I can reach no further back. Whatever could be given
I gave – ring-necked plover, red-throated loon,
nodding saxifrage. I see questions I thought must pass

pouring into the sea about the steadfastness
we survive in. I see their meaning, feel the claim,
wonder was the giving worth the gain?

Among the crosses on the hill, the wind makes in its throat
a leaving-taking for the flight of the arctic tern: *rise*
into a sky of milk into the long yet-to-come. Fly

from this colony of tin on frigid ground and I will follow.
We are one and we will keep as one, in thrall to the stern
come-hithering that turns the world.

NOTE

It is believed that female humpback whales make a patterned sound only; the whale song scientists currently refer to has been thus far only detected in males. On page 75, 'song' is used metaphorically.

Cloud

98 Before moon was torn away to what became the sky, before rains that filled the basins of the young world, before cloud.

Before cloud, the sun pulled molten liquids into tides unimpeded.

Before sun is too far to remember.

As soon as earth began to cool, clouds closed the world from the sun into darkness and all moisture that fell became steam.

As soon as steam rose it became cloud once more, the shape of the land and cavernous deeps could not be seen.

As soon as, in each case, took a very long time.

Now rain begins to fall and fall during what
could be called day and night as the sun shines pale
and watery light through the mist.
From cloud the rain descends unending on
continents, into the craters, dissolving rock, bearing
minerals away into rivers and bays, salting the water.
Beyond all else are clouds, their shadows
moving over granite.

Water leads it does not follow,
cares nothing for the long and short span of marvel.
Answers only to the moon,
downhill downhill all the way to ocean's surge
and pull, the breakers.

The surf rears high,
a foamy spillage tidal, turned, sweeps
in troughs and crestings,
over shoals, beds of snapping shrimp, lattice of silica
chambers, upswelling

over the glass sponge reef, the molten fissures
and moving plate, going going gone. Without a place
to hide,
now airborne, now falling free,
the many chapters of surf's one story: Beginning.

And the river went out of Eden
to water the garden.

Where once the river was, *101*
hang your harp
upon the willow.

It will come, the day
when only salt remains,
and there is nothing

save the flame of thirst.

Notes

Parts and portions of this book have appeared elsewhere and I am grateful to the editors and publishers: *Kingston Poets Gallery*, *Literary Review of Canada*, *'Scapes*, *The Salmon River Watershed.*

"Beloved of the Sky" is derived from the title of a painting by Emily Carr, Vancouver Art Gallery.

"Unlike Our Present Lives" arose from the WWI diary of Lawrence Hooey, aged seventeen, and is for his daughter Margaret.

The title "The Turning" is taken from a notebook of Gwen John, National Library of Wales.

"Unsigned, Under Glass" imagines the life of Harriet Clench, the wife of the painter Paul Kane.

Thanks to Helen Humphreys for the title. My gratitude to Beth Follett, maker of beautiful books, for her abiding faith in the necessity of poems. To Zab, for her genius. To Erín Moure, ardent reader and thinker, whose invention, love of mischief and absolute attention to words have made this book what it could be.

MARGARET McLAUCHLAN

JOANNE PAGE is the author of two previous books of poetry: *Persuasion for a Mathematician* (Pedlar Press, 2003), and *The River & The Lake* (Quarry Press, 1993). She lives in Kingston, Ontario.